AF498536

TABLE OF CONTENTS

INTRODUCTION 1

IN SEARCH OF ME 5

TAKE ACTION 29

POWER OF EMOTIONS 34

ROADMAP FROM VICTIM TO VICTOR 52

TOOLS AND TECHNIQUES TO REVEAL INFINITE

POTENTIAL 66

Introduction

"I feel so stressed/ I feel suffocated/ I feel confused"

"How to motivate myself towards achieving my goal?"

"I feel so lost. How to find my purpose?"

"I have everything, still, I don't feel happy"

"Why do people hurt me so much?"

"How to create a harmonious family?"

"Everybody around me is so demanding, how can I create peace in my life?"

"Why is Life so unfair to me always?

"Why can't the world be a better place to live in?"

"I wake up in the morning and I don't know what to do?"

"How to motivate myself towards achieving my goal?"

"I want to do something big, but where and how to start the journey?"

"How and where to find unlimited or absolute Joy?"

"How to become successful?"

If you resonate with any of these statements then you are at the right place and you are ready to achieve greater success in life. But how? Everybody says that thinking negatively is not good. You are right, you already know it but still can't stop negative thoughts hovering over you. This is totally natural as we all are humans after all, isn't it? But if you are reading this book it means you want to change your current situation, right? And you are ready to take the desired action.

So this book is for you **If You...**

* ❖ FEEL exhausted/weighed down/burnt out by life's responsibilities/social pressures.

* ❖ Feel that every day you are losing the battle to yourself and want to reclaim your older version- the one brimming with energy, passion, and a zest for life.

* ❖ Feeling challenges in the areas of Health, Finances, Relationships or overall well-being.

* ❖ Feel insecure and fearful about taking the next big step towards growth in life.

* ❖ Are putting your desires and passions under the carpet and acting as a puppet?

* ❖ Are done with compromising and you want to develop an "Abundance mindset"?

* ❖ Want more from life – more love, joy, passion, health, wealth, peace and abundance?

* ❖ Want to break free from the limiting beliefs that are holding you back?

* ❖ Want to live a life by being your authentic self?

* ❖ Want to serve society through your unique talents?

* ❖ Want to achieve breakthrough fast-track growth in your career by playing big?

* ❖ Want to develop Leadership qualities?

* ❖ ARE READY TO FEEL MORE CONNECTED with your deeper inner self AND AT PEACE WITH YOURSELF?

Such thoughts are the starting point to begin your amazing journey of transformation from a negative state of "Victim" to an amazing state of "Victor".

You are ready to become a WOW- Woman Of Wonders.

Who is Woman of Wonder- WOW?

She is the one who-

* ❖ Believes in herself and practices Self-love.

* ❖ Lives a life filled with passion and purpose.

* ❖ Receives abundance in all areas of life.

* ❖ Illuminates the world through their inner brilliance.

* ❖ Lives consciously through Self-control. by expanding her knowledge.

* ❖ Unapologetically, authentically unstoppable and much more!

Yes, you are our next WOW !!

Pat your back for holding onto life so far through all your struggles and challenges. You might have been in countless situations where life bogged you down with responsibilities and you have chosen others over your happiness. When you felt like having a last piece of cake but sacrificed for the sake of others' desires. Mark my words, ***"You have all the rights to live the most beautiful life of your dreams and desires."*** This book is your key to unlocking a world filled with an abundance of health, wealth, relationships, and spirituality. This book will equip you with proven tools and techniques to fulfill all your dreams and transform all your life's poison into medicine. Your life's troubles, challenges and difficulties will become raw material for building the foundation of a future filled with joy, love, peace and success in all areas of life. When you want to change but- familiar feels safe and change feels overwhelming. That is the right moment for you to take action.

This book is your handy guide to bringing 10x growth in all these areas of life through the power of the subconscious mind:

 ❖ Emotional management

 ❖ Healing

 ❖ Self-awareness

 ❖ Self-love

 ❖ Goal setting

 ❖ Time management

 ❖ Action plan

 ❖ Self-motivation and much more.

Practicing these techniques regularly will automatically propel you to take inspired actions to live each day purposefully towards fulfilling all your dreams and aspirations. Don't just skip through these chapters, it is a step-by-step process. To reap the maximum benefits in the most effective way, go chapter to chapter and finish the exercises one by one.

Wishing you all the best for starting this wonderful journey of self-exploration towards living purposeful life.

The purpose of life is to live a life of purpose

- Robert Byrne

In Search of ME

This amazing journey of your transformation starts with knowing your starting point. Most of the time we know our destination point: where we want to reach in life but we don't understand where we are currently. Oftentimes we are not sure about the path we should choose to reach our destination with happiness. So it is crucial to know yourself and understand your needs and your behaviors before beginning this magical journey of transforming dreams into reality. You are unique and your growth journey is also unique. Knowing yourself will help you to create your unique step-by-step plan to set up your milestones. This book will guide you at every step of your self-exploration and then strengthen you with the right tools and techniques to confidently complete your transformational journey.

1. Who am I?

The journey of transformation begins with knowing your current reality. Your life's events have a greater influence in shaping your personality and behaviors.

Have you ever asked yourself the most significant question of humankind: **WHO am I?**

This question has been answered with profundity by most of the religions, and philosophies across the world. Every answer to this question is correct in the perspective in which it is answered. There are no right or wrong answers.

At this point, pause for a minute and ask this question to yourself and focus on the inner voice coming from your heart.

<table>
<tr><td>

Question: Who am I?

Answer:_______________________________________

____

____

____

____

____

____

(please write down all your answers to this question in a notepad, in case this space is short)

</td></tr>
</table>

Now check your answers and see if it resonates with any of the following:

* I am who I want to become.
* I am what my past has made me.
* I am what I feel and think about myself.
* I am a product of my past situations.
* My life's challenges have made the person who I am.

Now, let's try to understand how a personality is developed.

As a human being grows in life with time, the 3 main factors responsible for the evolution are:

A) Genetics:

This describes the natural effects on your personality that are genetically transmitted from one generation to another. Not much can be done to change these features as they are inherited from one generation to another. For example, genetics impacts how you look. Apart from physical appearance, it may also affect some factors like your temperament and how you react to different situations, as well as your level of relaxation. It could potentially impact the social skills of children. It encompasses a range of factors including your social life, resilience, and narcissistic traits. Although these traits are unchangeable, they can be softened through continuous practice once you identify the traits you wish to work on.

B) Life Experiences:

Specific life events and experiences, such as trauma, loss, success, failure, achievements, and setbacks, can deeply impact your personality development and behavioral patterns. Your beliefs, values, and attitudes can be influenced by these experiences, shaping future choices and behavior.

Past traumas are the lasting emotional impacts of distressing events, affecting self-perception, safety, and emotional control. These experiences often leave individuals feeling ashamed, helpless, unsafe and scared. Despite these challenges, traumas have the capacity to foster personal growth and resilience, pushing you to develop coping and problem-solving skills. These tough experiences prompt deep self-reflection, leading to significant personal changes. Thus, while difficult, past traumas are essential for both personal and societal evolution. It eventually helps you build strength and resilience to face future challenges.

Success and achievements in the past strongly influence your beliefs about your abilities. When you succeed, you start to believe more in yourself, creating a positive cycle where confidence leads to more effort and further success. For example, a student who does well in a test might believe that he/she is good at that subject, motivating him/her to study more and keep doing well. This success boosts his/her self-confidence. Past triumphs help to see obstacles as temporary and manageable. Individual's victories can also inspire communities, creating a culture of confidence and achievement. However, it is important to balance this with learning from failures to avoid becoming overly cautious and resistant to new challenges.

C) Environment:

Your environment plays a pivotal role in your lives. It includes the settings where you live and grow, such as your home, school, workplace, society and other places where you spend significant time. The environment shapes your perspectives and behaviors from a young age. Environmental factors also encompass elements like languages, religions, and cultural practices that influence your daily experiences and growth. For instance, the languages you learn and the religious beliefs you are exposed to form the foundation of how you communicate and what you value. Cultural norms and practices you observe around teach you about acceptable behavior and social expectations. Even the physical aspects of your environment, like urban versus rural settings, can influence your hobbies, interests, and lifestyle choices. As you interact with your environment over time, it subtly guides your decisions, molds your values, and even affects your ambitions and career paths. Essentially, your environment is a key architect of your identity.

People are often said to be the "product of their environment." This refers to the idea that your personality is significantly shaped by above-cited factors. These factors act as raw materials in shaping your mental, physical, financial, social, and spiritual state of life. Although these factors have a deep-rooted impact on your personality. But at the same time, the power to transform it in the desired direction also lies in your hands.

Just ask yourself how you feel about defining yourself currently in terms of who you intrinsically are. Is it based on the parameters of how society defines you or wants you to be/ is it based on past conditioning / is it based on patterns created through your reactions to life's hardships?

Question: After having the above knowledge, how do you define yourself?

Answer:____

____

____

____

____

____

____

(Please use a notepad to write down your answer to this question if this space is short)

2. A) Who I want to be ?

Considering 'Who I Want to Be' means thinking about the person you aspire to become. It is about envisioning your future version and setting goals to achieve that. This contemplation will help you understand what is important to you and what makes you happy. Whether it is being helpful, creative, brave, successful, fearless, joyful, skillful etc. it is about finding your own path and becoming the best version of you. Exploring 'Who I Want to Be' is like creating a map for your life, guiding you towards a future filled with living a more meaningful life aligned with your own goals and purpose.

Now the question arises- How do you know what your purpose in life is?

Answers to the below questions will help you to get some insights to your search for your noble mission and purpose in life:

Table-1:

Sl. no.	Question	Answer
1	What are the practices that you don't like to see being done wrong?	
2	What are you passionate about? What do you love doing (think about your hobbies or something that you can do till midnight without feeling tired at all)	

3	What comes easily and naturally to you?	
4	What are your greatest 5 gifts/qualities? (take the help of your friends and family to understand this)	
5	How can you use your passion/s to serve others?	

Answers to these questions will give you a framework to understand the unique qualities and talents with which the Universe has gifted you. Your purpose in life is to serve the world through your innate uniqueness.

The greatest joy and contentment is felt in life when you feel - "I am who I want to become."

2. B) How to start the journey of living a purposeful life?

This journey of living a joyful life starts with inculcating faith in your infinite potential. While living your life under the impact of the 3 factors mentioned above, you tend to forget your true powers to live a peaceful and meaningful life. Sometimes these 3 factors create some mental wounds and force to accept the reality perceived through their lenses. The hurt created thus controls your behavior and blocks your progress. Therefore, it becomes utterly important to heal all such wounds so that your soul can move forward in the direction of self-growth. The wounds make you feel bad about yourself. It may make you believe that there is something missing in you, that you are not good enough, or you are not flawless. There is nothing like a perfect person exists, it is just a negative thought arising in your head when you compare yourself to others. Please remember that these scars can be healed with care and self-love, ultimately allowing you to enhance the beauty of your soul.

Let's understand this healing process through the concept of Kintsugi (Meaning "joining with gold"):

Pic source: https://creativecommons.org/licenses/by-nc/3.0/

An ancient Japanese art of embracing imperfection. This centuries-old art is more than an aesthetic. It is part of a broader philosophy of embracing the beauty of human flaws.

Learn to accept yourself as it is without being too critical about your flaws (either perceived by others or by you).

Exercise: Write down the top 10 things about yourself which you/ others don't like.

*Answer:*____

____

____

____

____

____

Now, use the below table to identify if these narratives are created by you or others. Check if it is still valid as some of these might have been created in your childhood/ or long ago, but you are still carrying its burden in your heart.

Table-2:

Sl. no	Things that you/ others don't like about you	Is it still valid? Do I still carry it?	Do I want to change it?
1			
2			
3			
4			
5			
6			

7			
8			
9			
10			

Now, separately compile all the points with an answer "No" in the below table:

<u>Table-3:</u>

List of all the "Nos"	The new perspective to look at these statements*
	These are other people's perceptions about me which do not belong to me anymore. I have completely transformed myself and do not identify with any of these anymore. Now I am completely free from the older version of me and I am ready to transform into a newer and better version of me.

*: Repeat this statement several times a day aloud by looking in the mirror or in your heart to free yourself.

3. Create a new "You" to become who you want to be, begin the process now:

A) Your dream life:

"Enough is enough!! Now I want to live a life that I had always envisioned for myself." if this is how you are feeling currently then congratulations! You are ready to take action towards your overall transformation. This awareness about understanding your deep desire to live a life filled with love, joy, success, hope, happiness, peace, good health, wealth, luxury, and spirituality through purposeful living is your first milestone in this journey of transformation through introspection and self-growth.

Now, from the above exercise separately compile all the points with an answer "YES" in the below table:

Table-4:

List of all the "Yes"	The new perspective to look at these statements*
	I am ready to give a new meaning to these perceptions about me either created by me or by others. I am ready to take transformative actions to create a much better life by unleashing my infinite potential. The life that I have always envisioned for myself and that I truly deserve.

If all your "Yes" are not enough to propel you in improving your life condition, let's do another exercise to go even deeper in your subconscious mind:

Exercise: Find a quiet and comfortable space where you won't be disturbed. If possible, create a serene atmosphere for relaxation and reflection. You can listen to any healing music to begin this exercise and keep a pen and notepad near you. Close your eyes and bring your awareness to the present moment through five to ten deep belly breaths. Release all the stress in your body and relax your mind with every exhale. Envision yourself living your dream life, filled with all the elements you desire – joy, success, hope, happiness, peace, good health, wealth, luxury, spirituality, and purpose. Imagine every aspect of your life unfolding exactly as you wish it to be. Picture yourself waking up in the morning feeling fulfilled and excited about the day ahead. Visualize the environment around you, the people you interact with, and the activities you engage in. Allow yourself to immerse fully in this vision. After a while, gradually come back to your current state and open your eyes.

Now write down your reflections on the following questions:

Question: Who am I in my dream life? Describe the qualities, characteristics, and values that define the person you aspire to be.

*Answer:*____

____

____

____

Question: What brings the most joy and fulfillment in this envisioned life?

Answer:____

____

____

____

____

____

Question: How do you define success and purpose in your dream life?

Answer:____

____

____

____

____

____

The answers to these questions will create a strong foundation for building a greater life for yourself.

Creating your destiny through living an empowered life:

Live life to explore your infinite potential as a human being and know that you have the power of the universe as this practice will let the hidden power embrace your thoughts. Below is the step-by-step method to start working on creating the most beautiful life. Fill in the tables below for each area of life with honesty and the results will give you a direction for moving up in life.

<u>Table-5:</u>

Area of Life	People I admire and see as my role model	What quality I admire in them
Health (Physical & Mental)		
Wealth (including career)		
Relationships (with self & others)		
Spirituality (for self and serving others)		

Self-growth is a step-by-step constant process which requires focused efforts and perseverance. As the next step, pick only 3 qualities from the above table on which you want to focus right now for the next 6 months:

Table-6

Sl. no.	Quality from the above table that you want to imbibe	Quantification parameters	Your current level (A)	Desired level in six months (B)
1				
2				
3				
(sample)	Health (Physical)- My role model has his/ her ideal body weight and shape	Weight- Ideal as per BMI Exercise- minimum 45mins daily. Diet- Healthy food daily	Weight- more as per BMI. Exercise- No exercise. Diet- Healthy	Weight- __Kg.. Exercise- Min. 30 mins daily. Diet- Healthy with a maximum of 1 cheat day per week.

Above soul searching will help you to define your origin point (Column-A) and destination point (Column-B) in the journey of your self-transformation to your dream life. Tools and techniques to achieve the desired levels are explained in detail in Chapter- 5.

Once you achieve your desired levels, these exercises are to be repeated to work on developing other qualities from Table-5. These exercises should be done periodically (six monthly/ yearly) so that you can align yourself to your dreams and desires.

B) Live motivated life consistently:

Live an active life but not reactive (free from the shackles of others' perceptions about you). How to maintain a highly motivated life state working towards achieving the purpose of life? What to do when you don't know what you want? You want to connect to your higher purpose in life, created by the creator but you are not aware of it. You don't even know what you are passionate about and what gives you absolute joy. And sometimes even if you know your passion, you are clueless about how to stay motivated through challenges in life? The best way to live a motivated life is by becoming your best friend. Yes, you read it right, YOU HAVE TO BECOME YOUR BEST FRIEND.

Just recall a time when you motivated some of your good friends when they were depressed. Learn to talk to yourself in the same manner. You are with yourself 24/7. You listen to all the chatter happening in your mind all the time. So it is a great idea to become your best friend and treat yourself in the same way you did to help someone to heal. Imagine how great it would be, as you are the only person on this earth who will be with you till your last breath.

Living a motivated life is about finding the inner drive and passion that propels you forward, inspiring you to pursue your goals with determination and enthusiasm. It is like starting every day with a purpose, ready to face challenges and seize opportunities. Motivation drives your actions, leading to personal growth, success, and fulfillment. Your unwavering belief in yourself and your vision for the future pushes you forward with every step you take. Despite obstacles or setbacks, your motivation remains unwavering, pushing you to persevere and overcome any hurdles in your path. You cultivate a mindset of positivity and resilience, viewing failures as learning experiences and using them to fuel your continued progress. By living a motivated life, you tap into your inner strength and drive to turn your dreams into reality, understanding that with commitment and persistence, everything becomes achievable.

Develop the following qualities to foster a motivation mindset:

I.   **Growth:**

Focus on self growth & self love. Always stay focused on the larger purpose of your goal of achieving growth by creating value in others' lives. Creating value simply means that you help others when they need you. This process will help you to learn from your experiences in the journey of growth.

II.   **Commitment:**

Commit to yourself. Always remember, a 1000-mile journey starts with one single step. So commit to starting the journey by taking small steps. Break down bigger goals into smaller goals and achieve them through staying committed to making consistent efforts. Always remember that consistency is the key.

III.   **Celebrate every win:**

Whenever you achieve a milestone, big or small, celebrate it by congratulating yourself. Remember, every win is important! Use every victory to boost your confidence. Appreciation is a small word but appears with great results.

IV.   Perseverance:

This is the most important step. Many people start the journey but cannot persevere and lose motivation. Keep reminding yourself of the Big "WHY"- the critical reason for you to begin this journey. Remember all the wins that you have achieved so far and push yourself by reminding yourself: "The best is yet to come". Keep going, no matter what.

C) What is stopping you from living your dream life:

Let's dive deep into your life and figure out the intrinsic reasons from your past lives that are stopping you from living the life of your dreams. Let's dissect further and see if these mental limitations are created by others/ Society / external factors/ your conditioning or just your limiting beliefs. Sit in quiet and listen to the excuse/narrative/stories you are telling yourself for not living your dream life. For example: start with " **I want** to become a YouTuber **BUT** I don't have time-" or **I want** to own a business, **BUT** I don't know how to do it".

Write 5 such points around your goals and see what excuses you are giving to yourself for not taking action towards achieving it:

1. I want_________________, but _________________

2. I want_________________, but _________________

3. I want_________________, but _________________

4. I want_________________, but _________________

5. I want_________________, but _________________

Now check your answers and see which of the following most common "buts" have held you back in the past.

But, it's too hard.

But, it'll take too long.

But, I don't have time.

But, it's too risky.

But, it's overwhelming etc....

Now try to analyze the core Limiting Beliefs attached to these "But" statements. What does it cumulatively indicate, choose from the below list or create your own list of 5 such critical beliefs about yourself that are stopping you from fulfilling your dreams in life?

Look for the most central beliefs to your sense of identity and are the most important aspects of your life's story so far.

1) I am not good enough

2) I am not perfect.

3) I am not worthy of love.

4) I am not worthy of respect.

5) I am not worthy of care and support.

6) I lack something.

7) I am not good-looking.

8) I am not talented enough.

9) I do not deserve good things in life.

10) I am not worthy of appreciation.

Then for each of the 5 Core Beliefs, ask yourself the following questions:

Question: What story do you tell? (what words do you say to yourself or others say about it?)

*Answer:*____

____

____

____

Question: Where (or who) did this belief come from?

*Answer:*____

____

____

____

Question: Is it true? How do you know?

*Answer:*____

____

____

____

Question: Are you absolutely sure?

*Answer:*____

____

____

____

Question: How do you feel when you think about this belief (or tell this story to yourself)?

*Answer:*____

____

____

____

Question: Who would you be without this belief or story?

*Answer:*____

____

____

____

Question: How can it be told differently?

*Answer:*____

____

____

____

Question: What do you WANT to believe? (If you aren't sure about what you would prefer to believe, try writing out 5 different ways of thinking about it. Then, ask yourself "how do I feel about the original belief now? Do any of the new ones feel more true?)

*Answer:*____

____

____

____

For each excuse you commonly use, write 5 positive affirmation statements. For example, change "I don't have time" to "I make time for what is important to me."

1.____

2.____

3.____

4.____

5.____

Unhealed past experiences:

Unhealed past experiences are like old wounds that haven't fully healed. They can be things that hurt you long ago, such as a bad argument with a friend, losing someone close, or being treated unfairly. Even after a long time, these memories can still affect how you feel and act today. If you don't address these old wounds, they might make you feel scared, sad, or angry without a clear reason. A couple of times you are left with invisible scars in your heart. Such experiences are to be healed so that you can live in peace. Healing these experiences often involves talking about them, maybe with friends, family, or a counselor, and learning to understand and forgive yourself and others. This helps you move forward happier and healthier. The complete healing cannot be covered in the scope of this book as it involves healing at several levels. However some exercises given in Chapter 5 will help to achieve healing at some level.

To move one step towards healing, try the following activity (which might appear difficult to do initially. But believe me, it will free your heart and mind from all the negativity around that pain):

Close your eyes and identify 3 people in your life who are responsible for pain in your life. Now decide to apply the formula of "No A B C":

"A": Accusation:

Whatever happens to you, do not accuse anyone for your current situation. At any moment when this idea of accusing others comes into your mind, take a few deep breaths and replace it with the thought that you are responsible for all your life's experiences. Then release all your negative thoughts by wishing peace & joy in your life and in the life of accused people.

"B": Blame:

Whenever the urge to blame others arises, pause and remind yourself that blaming others will not reduce the hurt caused to you. At any moment when you catch yourself in a state of blaming others, take a few deep breaths and replace it with the thought that you are responsible for all your life's experiences. Then release all your negative thoughts by wishing peace & joy in your life and in the life of accused people.

"C": Complain:

Although it may seem productive, complaining usually does little to solve problems. At any moment when you catch yourself in a state of blaming others, take a few deep breaths and replace it with the thought that you are responsible for all your life's experiences. Feel happy about having the power to change your current reality.

Then release all your negative thoughts by wishing peace & joy in your life and in the life of accused people.

Wonderful results are achieved if you can apply this policy of "NO ABC" in your daily lives.

So from now onwards, you have to free yourself from accusing, blaming or complaining about these people. And eventually, you will see that you have completely stopped accusing, blaming and complaining about anyone in your life, whether you like them or not. It may take some time to reach this stage, but trust me, it is a happy place. Your heart and mind will feel light as it is free from any hatred or negativity for anyone.

Life is not about knowing yourself,
life is about creating yourself.

- George Bernard shaw.

Take Action

नियतं कुरु कर्म त्वं कर्म ज्यायो ह्यकर्मणः

(niyataṁ kuru karma tvaṁ karma jyāyo hyakarmaṇ aḥ)

Bhagavad Gita: Chapter 3, Verse 8

Perform your prescribed duty, for action is better than inaction.

As stated in the above shloka of Bhagavad Geeta, taking action is better than doing nothing. Even during the darkest phase of your life, when you continue to take actions towards your goals, your victory is certain.

When you act, you steer your life towards success and fulfillment. Inaction keeps you stuck and often leads to missed chances and regrets. By taking determined actions, you take control of your life and create a brighter future. Always remember, your destiny is in your hands; act now to create it in the most beautiful manner!!

How to take the first step when you are already so scared and feeling under confident?

To fully utilize the power of your actions, and become a WOW-Woman Of Wonders, take action as per the below definition:

A- Aim- Aim higher always.

C- Clarity, courage, consistency.

T- Trust the process.

I- Intention- Set the right intention.

O-Openness- Be open to the ideas aligned to self-growth.

N- No- Learn to say "No" to everything that is not aligned with your idea of life.

Aim- Aim higher always:

Always keep your dreams higher. Sometimes you shine a little less so that people around can bear the light you emit. Please never dim your shine. You are carrying the energy of the Universe. You have got the power, you have to just unleash it. Your Ambitions fuel the process of doing better and bigger things in life. So always set your sights higher; aim beyond what seems possible. When you aim higher, you challenge yourself to grow and achieve greater things. Strive for excellence, not mediocrity. Let your aspirations drive you towards success and fulfillment in every endeavor.

C- Clarity, courage, consistency:

Clarity provides direction, courage fuels determination, and consistency ensures progress. Together, they empower you to take the right actions. With clarity of purpose, the courage to pursue it, and through perseverance, you can overcome every obstacle and achieve your goals. Constantly polish these virtues to create an indomitable spirit to navigate challenges and realize your aspirations with confidence.

Identify your skills, and focus more on personal growth. Identify your strengths and align them with your goals. Continue polishing your skills and if required, work on your weaknesses to bring more alignment of your actions towards your goals and vision. Create a larger-than-life vision for yourself with the larger purpose of serving humanity. Once you begin with a clear perspective, no one can stop you from achieving your goals.

T- Trust the process:

"Trust the process", is the mantra for navigating life's uncertainties. It is about surrendering to the journey, and embracing its twists and turns with faith. Sometimes progress isn't linear; always remember all your setbacks are stepping stones, not roadblocks. Every experience shapes you, creating resilience and wisdom. Have patience; growth takes time. Trusting the process means believing in your path, even when it is blurred. It is a reminder to stay committed, knowing that every effort, no matter how small, contributes to your evolution. So, when doubts arise, breathe, and trust. In the end, the process unveils the beauty of your transformation.

I- Intention- Set the right intention:

The most important thing is to set the right intention, as it influences your actions and results. It involves aligning your thoughts, desires, and actions with your core values and aspirations. Having clear intentions helps you live purposefully and pursue meaningful endeavors. When you have genuine and sincere intentions, your efforts bear fruit and create a positive impact on the world. Whether in relationships, work, or personal growth, the right intention infuses your endeavors with authenticity and integrity. It serves as a compass, guiding you towards fulfillment and aligning you with the greater good. So, set your intention wisely, for it shapes your destiny.

O-Openness- Be open to the ideas aligned to self growth:

Being open to ideas that help you grow is crucial for personal growth. It means being ready to explore new perspectives, accept change, and question what you believe. By remaining receptive, you invite opportunities for learning and transformation into your life. Whether it is from reading, mentors, or experiences, every idea you encounter helps you evolve. Openness builds resilience, adaptability, and self-awareness. It empowers you to reach your potential, overcome limits, and live a more fulfilling life. So, keep an open mind; curiosity and receptivity fuel growth. Embracing new ideas encourages you to be innovative and creative, seeing challenges as chances to learn and grow towards self-fulfillment. Through openness, you cultivate a growth mindset, seeing obstacles as opportunities for learning and growth. So, welcome new ideas with curiosity and enthusiasm, for they hold the potential to propel you towards greater fulfillment and self-actualization. Openness lets you leave behind the rigidity of negative thoughts that clenched you behind the shackles.

N- No- Learn to say "No" to everything that is not aligned with your idea of life:

Learning to say "No" to anything that is not aligned with your life's vision is essential for self-care and authenticity. It is about setting boundaries and prioritizing your well-being and values. By declining commitments or relationships that don't serve you, you preserve your energy and focus on what truly matters. Saying "No" empowers you to stay true to yourself, fostering self-respect and confidence. It is a declaration of self-responsibility, guiding you towards a life in harmony with your aspirations. Embrace the power of "No" to honor your priorities and create space for growth, fulfillment, and the realization of your dreams.

Avoid taking actions from a place of blame, shame, judgment, guilt, and fear; rather take actions from a place of faith and self-love.

Even when you feel that you cannot go out in the field of your interest due to lack of time, money, energy, resources or your readiness to take that plunge. That is the appropriate time for you to do your HOMEWORK- upskill yourself, and do the research. Carve a strong foundation for all your future battles, surround yourself with positive people, listen to motivating podcasts, read books, and enroll for free courses in the field of your interest.

3

Power of Emotions

If you are reading this book, congratulations! Pat your back, as you have made a strong decision to take action to transform your life from "Victim" to "Victor". This powerful decision is your first step towards monumental victories in your life. This decision backed up with determined actions will help you to use your infinite potential and live a life like a victor under any challenging situations or adversities.

For this, you will have to go deeper and listen to your own thoughts and emotions.

What are emotions? Emotions can be defined in many ways, but to put it in simple words, it is a natural instinctive state of mind deriving from one's circumstances, mood, learning from past experiences or relationships with others. There are 6 basic types of emotions / emotional energies that you can feel in your lives:

1. Happiness

2. Sadness

3. Fear

4. Anger

5. Disgust

6. Surprise

In this chapter you will understand how your emotions are energy in motion and how you can use this powerful force of this energy, already existing in your life to live a happy and abundant life. You have to learn the art of letting the emotions flow freely so that you can channelise their energy in alignment with your goals rather than allowing them to create blockages in your lives.

The aim is to develop emotional resilience and increase emotional intelligence. You often expect others to understand your emotions but fail to understand yourself. You should not let the key to your emotions in other's hands to remain happy, rather should take charge of yourselves.

At a metaphysical level, everything is matter and every particle vibrates at a certain frequency. Dr. Joe Dispenza, a neuroscientist, author, and speaker, has also studied the connection between thoughts, feelings, and biology- "Thoughts produce an electrical charge, while feelings produce a magnetic charge. This energy interacts with the quantum field, producing an effect on the environment. Therefore, it is essential to have positive thoughts and emotions as they produce positive energy that can make positive contributions to life.

To simplify, emotions, thoughts, actions and reality are directly related to each other. For example, when you feel sad or low, your energy levels go down, whereas whenever you feel inspired and happy, your body feels energized. This is also true vice-versa, whenever you do some form of physical exercise like yoga, brisk walk, running or dancing, your mood is uplifted and you feel refreshed and recharged.

Those who understand this relationship of cause and effect between emotions/ thoughts and physical reality are the game changers. They are the people who have got the key to the biggest secret of the workings of this world. These people know how they can create the desired reality by controlling their emotions and thoughts and through conscious living. The "cause" is created using the power of words, thoughts and emotions to create the "effect" of the desired reality.

Taking a step back and developing the ability to navigate through your emotions, more so when others' emotions are also involved is the biggest power that you possess. Choose your choices wisely.

Know your emotional state / be aware of your emotions:

Now you have understood that your thoughts and emotions have a direct link to your physical reality. Knowing your emotions is the first step towards using their power to your benefit.

How can you use this principle when you are feeling low and sad? Check your affordability of negative emotions, and ask this question to yourself; if I can afford this low life-state? It requires constant practice to keep undesired thoughts in check and to create the desired positive thoughts regularly.

It is like taking a mental shower every day to keep your mental space clean and tidy so that creative and productive ideas can be flourished there.

Don't give a piece of your "peace of Mind" to anyone or everyone.

So at every moment of life, you are in one of the six states of emotions as referred to above. There are no bad or good emotions. Please understand every emotion carries some energy and it is your body's way of making you aware of your reactions to the changes happening around us.

Every emotion carries a message, if you are able to decode that message then you can harness the energy in that emotion by channeling in the direction of your goals.

A) 3 'As' for channeling the emotional energy:

This is a 3-step process to channeling the emotional energy.

Step-1: ACKNOWLEDGE:

Acknowledge your emotions. Acknowledging your emotions means recognizing what you're feeling at any given time. Embrace your mental state like a good friend. Just like you wouldn't ignore a friend, don't ignore your feelings. Do not observe yourself critically, rather identify the correct emotion. Ask yourself this question: Am I feeling happy, sad, fearful, angered, disgusted or surprised? Think about where it might be coming from. This step is important because understanding your emotions can help you respond to them better. You have been told that negative emotions are not right and you should not feel/ express them quite often. But I would suggest being true to yourself and acknowledging your emotions as it is. Don't try to put away any emotion that you feel is not right. Be open to understanding your emotions in their truest form. Developing a habit of always acknowledging your emotions develops a greater level of understanding yourself better and making healthy choices.

This is the first step towards cultivating the habit of self-love by valuing your own emotions and feelings.

Step-2: ACCEPT:

Accepting your emotions means understanding that it is okay to feel whatever you're feeling without judging yourself. Sometimes you feel happy, sad, angry, or scared, and that's all normal. Instead of hiding these feelings or being upset with yourself for having them, you should acknowledge them. This doesn't mean you have to like what you're feeling, but rather letting yourself experience the emotion fully. Recognizing your emotions can help you handle them better. When you accept your feelings, you can be kinder to yourself and learn more about why you feel the way you do. This makes it easier to deal with tough situations and helps you get along better with others. Every emotion is an expression of how you are feeling, and it is important to allow yourself to feel them. When you accept your emotions, you stop fighting with them and start learning from them, which can lead to greater emotional balance and strength.

Step-3: ADDRESSAL:

Address your emotions- Addressing your emotions means taking action once you have acknowledged and accepted them. This could involve figuring out what triggers certain emotions and thinking about how to handle these feelings in a healthy way. If you're feeling sad, perhaps you could talk to a friend or write down your thoughts. If you're angry, maybe physical exercise or deep breathing could help. Addressing your emotions isn't about getting rid of them; it is about managing how they affect your life. Taking these steps can help you feel more in control and can improve your overall emotional well-being.

B) I have emotions, I am not my emotions:

"In Irish, when you talk about an emotion, you don't say, 'I am sad.' You'd say, 'Sadness is on me – Ta' Bron Orm.' I love that because there's an implication of not identifying yourself with the emotion fully. I am not sad, it is just that sadness is on me for a while. Something else will be on me another time, and that's a good thing to recognize." -Pádraig Ó Tuama (Irish poet and theologian)

This allows you to take charge of our emotional state by using the power of words. This phrase indicates that I have the power to allow this emotion to cling to me for whatever duration I want it to be with me. The moment I decide to turn it around, I will be able to do that.

C) Emotional patterns:

Identify the negative loop of your most commonly occurring emotion and what is it reflecting (limiting beliefs)?

How to identify it? Do you like it? Do you want to continue to live with this pattern or do you want to change it?

Ask yourself- What do I want? And what action am I taking towards achieving whatever I want in life?

When you notice the same negative emotion popping up a lot, like anxiety, anger or sadness, it is important to identify what's causing it to keep coming back. This is like a negative loop. For instance, you might get angry every time you're running late because it makes you feel rushed and stressed. Recognizing this pattern is the first step. Once you know what triggers your anger, you can start working on ways to break the loop. Maybe wake up a bit earlier or organize your things the night before. By changing your routine, you can stop the cycle of getting angry and feel more at peace.

If you often find yourself feeling a certain negative emotion, like frustration or worry, it is helpful to spot the pattern or loop causing it. For example, if you worry a lot, you might notice it happens mostly when you're facing uncertain situations. Understanding this pattern is key. Next, think about small changes you can make to reduce your worry, like planning ahead or talking about your fears with someone you trust. Breaking the loop isn't about ignoring your feelings but managing them better. By recognizing and adjusting how you handle these situations, you can reduce the hold this emotion has on you.

Emotional patterns are like habits of feelings that keep coming up again and again in your lives. For example, if you often find yourself feeling nervous before meeting new people, there might be a pattern in how you handle social situations. These patterns often reflect deeper beliefs you hold about yourself, which are sometimes limiting and negative.

Let's say you always feel nervous and think, "I'm not interesting enough to talk to." This is a limiting belief because it puts you down and stops you from enjoying social interactions. It is like a little voice in your head telling you that you can't do something or you're not good enough, which isn't true. Everyone has something unique about them, including you.

How to come out of the loop of negative emotions:

Sometimes, you may feel like you are addicted to emotions which you don't like, such as sadness or worry. As a result of stress, anxiety or fear, these feelings keep coming back almost like a habit. It is difficult to come out of it because they appear familiar. And even though they don't make you happy, they create a sense of comfort zone just because of familiarity. Recognizing this pattern is the first step to liberate yourself from the vicious cycle of negativity. By noticing when and why these feelings emerge, and then learning healthier ways to respond/ manage you can develop a stronger emotional and mental health.

A) Negative thinking/ thinking too much about the past or future:

Constantly thinking about the past or worrying about the future can lead to negative thinking. When you focus too much on mistakes you've made or bad things that might happen, it can make you feel stressed or sad. It is like you're stuck in a loop that keeps you from enjoying the present. To break free from this cycle, try to focus more on what is happening right now. Remember, you can't change the past and the future hasn't happened yet, so try to enjoy today.

B) Lack of focus, distractions, and Procrastination:

Lack of focus, distractions, and procrastination are common problems that lead you to stay in the loop of negativity. Lack of focus can make it hard to stick with tasks long enough to finish them. You need to always remind yourself of the "Why you are doing it" to stay focussed on achieving your goal. Sometimes when the task appears difficult or time taking you tend to get trapped in distractions. Distractions give you temporary feelings of satisfaction, but in the long run you may feel that you have wasted your time, energy & resources on such activities. It needs a greater force to break through this pattern, and sometimes taking even a small action may look like a giant task. When actions appear daunting or difficult, you tend to delay. Procrastination is the delay of duties necessary to stay aligned with your goals. Be determined to break through the shackles of procrastination by adopting the tools & techniques given in the later chapters of this book for managing distractions.

C)   Comfort zone:

The psychological meaning as per Wikipedia is:

A comfort zone is a familiar psychological state where people are at ease and (perceive they are) in control of their environment, experiencing low levels of anxiety and stress.

It is a place or situation where you feel safe and familiar, at ease and without stress or worry. It is a place where you love to stay and avoid new or challenging things. While it feels nice to stay inside, it can also hold you back from growing and experiencing new adventures. Most of the time greater opportunities await just outside the comfort zone. Stepping out of your comfort zone means trying new activities, meeting new people, or facing fears. It can be scary at first, but it is how you learn and grow. Pushing your boundaries helps you build confidence and discover new abilities you never knew you had, making life more exciting and fulfilling. Idling in your comfort zones would never let you embrace the power that you have within. For finding yourself and your purpose, you need to step out of it and nothing can stop you from shining brilliantly in the world.

It is surprising to know that sometimes your unhappy place becomes your comfort zone as it gives you certainty and familiarity.

How to channelise my emotional energy:

Identify the emotion (use the table given below) and the root cause: Table for identification of the message your emotion is trying to give.

Emotion Identification Chart:

Below are 6 common emotions and descriptions of the emotion, physiological state, and common resulting behaviors. This chart will help you get a general idea of the signs and symptoms of each emotion to make them easier to identify; specifically, easier to identify early. Keep in mind everyone experiences each emotion at a different level and you may not experience all of the characteristics.

Table-7:

Emotion	Feelings/ Characteristics	Physical State	Behavior
Happiness	Positive feelings of well-being, happiness, delight, joy, gratitude, and mental clarity.	Head held high (posture), wide-eyed, smiling, laughing, grinning, relaxed and open body language.	Pleasant voice, friendly, at ease, easy going, forgiving.

Boredom	Unpleasant feelings of apathy, restlessness, indifference, emptiness.	Low energy, slumped posture, smirk or frown, low eyes, shallow breathing.	Resting head, fidgeting, staring.
Anxiety	Vague, unpleasant feelings of distress, uneasiness, worry, stress, nervousness,	Restlessness, sweating, hunched shoulders, swallowing, shallow breath, butterflies in the stomach, nausea.	Pacing, biting lip, fidgeting. Irritability, hypervigilance.
Anger	Feelings of hostility and hurt, out of control. Thoughts of blame and resentment. Irrational thinking.	Muscle tension, headache, increased heart rate & blood pressure, heavy breathing, clenched fist & jaw, trembling, red eyes.	Loud voice, yelling, cursing, sarcasm, pacing, aggression.

Sadness	Pain and sorrow, guilt, unworthiness, disappointmen t, helplessness, loss, grief,	Slumped posture and hunched shoulders, long face, slow movements , body aches, crying, shaking, fatigue, monotone voice.	Curling up into a ball, laying around, withdrawing, irritability.
Fear	Intense feeling of dread, or panic due to a perceived threat	Increased heart rate and pressure, alert eyes, high eyebrows, clammy, sweating, faster breath, goosebump s, shaky voice.	Freezing, fleeing, hiding.

Negative Emotion:

Negative emotions are feelings like sadness, anger, anxiety, fear, or jealousy that don't feel good. Everyone experiences these emotions, and they're a normal part of life. They can be uncomfortable, but they're important because they tell you when something might be wrong or when you need to make some changes. For example, feeling sad might show you that you need more support, while anger could signal that something isn't fair. It is important not to ignore these feelings or push them away. These emotions hover over you a little strongly but they are there to understand yourself a little better and find out ways to jump out of them as soon as possible. Try to understand what they're telling you and learn how to manage them in healthy ways.

Exercise:

How to reframe Negative Experiences and change the narrative you attach to it. Check yourself. What are your narratives? Understand your fundamental truth:

Think about any incident that made you feel frustrated, sad, angry, or disappointed; ask yourself the following questions:

Question: "What else might be going on here?"

*Answer:*____

____

____

____

Question: "What did I learn from this experience?"

*Answer:*____

____

____

____

Question: "What can I do differently next time?"

*Answer:*_______________________________________

____

____

____

Question: "What positive outcome eventually came as a result of this situation?

*Answer:*_______________________________________

____

____

____

Question: "What meaning does it have? What purpose does it give me?"

*Answer:*_______________________________________

____

____

____

Question: "How can I use this for GOOD?"

*Answer:*_______________________________________

____

____

____

Answers to these questions will help you reframe the narrative from a negative to a strengthening one by bringing out the lesson that you learnt through such experiences.

Positive Emotion:

Energy is neither created nor destroyed, it simply changes its form. Transmuting energy is your hidden power. Transmutation is transforming the energy of negative emotions that weigh you down into positive energies that uplift and enlighten you. You have the innate ability to shift your energies from one form to another form. When you learn the skill of transmuting energy, you master the ability to create your own authentic reality that you truly desire. Ways to achieve this are: breathing exercises, physical exercise, meditation, creative expression- art, dance, music, nature connection, affirmations & mantras, sound healing, emotional release techniques. Few of these techniques are explained in detail in later chapters of the book.

How to cleanse the emotional baggage from the past:

Carrying emotional baggage from the past can weigh you down and keep you away from living fully in the present. The most surprising fact is that you don't realize that this mental baggage can be blocking your growth in all areas of life. Cleansing this mental baggage helps free up emotional space, making room for new experiences and feelings. It can improve your mental health, relationships, and overall happiness, allowing you to move forward lighter and happier. This allows you to open the pathways to new opportunities and you learn to expand your capabilities

A)   Take responsibility for your actions: Taking responsibility for your actions is crucial because it shapes who you truly are. When you own up to what you do, whether good or bad, it helps you to learn from your mistakes and celebrate your successes. Both successes and failures are crucial to build a strong character. Success gives you confidence in your capabilities and failures teach you to learn something new or adopt a new way to your goal. Being responsible also builds trust with others, as others know that they can rely on you to be honest and accountable. By consistently taking responsibility, you grow stronger in character, build higher self-esteem and gain more control over your lives.

B) Cleansing techniques: Everyday you clean your physical body by brushing your teeth, by taking a shower and by washing your hands regularly. Have you pondered, how many times do you clean your mental body? You would agree that a lot of mental garbage is created day-in and day out either by your own negative thoughts or by others dumping their negativity on you. Now you know that your mind has a deep impact on your overall well-being. It is explained in this book how your thoughts can help you create the desired reality. Following exercise can help you create a clean mental space to be used for developing a foundation for building a beautiful future life.

I.   **Letter writing**- Sit at a quiet place, and take a few deep breaths. Take a notepad, and write a letter to the person/situation troubling you. Pour all your negative emotions and all your feelings around this. Write till you feel nothing is left in your heart around this person/ situation. Now immediately burn these sheets. Once all the papers are burned completely and cooled off, collect the ashes into your palms and either go to any open space (like backyard/park/riverside etc.) and blow out the ashes in the open sky and say" I release myself from these negative emotions, thank you, thank you, thank you" if you don't find open space, you can flush the ashes in the sink.

II.   Journaling your emotions about the situation: Sit in a quiet place, and take a few deep breaths. Take a notepad, and start writing about how you are feeling right now. Write down everything that comes to your mind. Just go with the flow, don't judge any of your feelings and emotions. Even if you feel like crying, continue pouring all your emotions and all your feelings without judging yourself. Write till you feel nothing is left in your heart. A time will come when your heart will start feeling light and very light, you can stop writing then. After this, close the notepad and repeat three times: "I have emotions, but I am not my emotion. I have the power to change my life, I love myself."

III.   Throw it out of your system: You can use any mirror for this exercise. Stand /sit in front of a mirror and talk to yourself, as you would talk to your best friend. Express all your emotions and feelings. Just let it out, whatever you are feeling at the moment. Once you feel that you are done with speaking to yourself in the mirror, nothing more is left to say. Wash your face and firmly say this to yourself: I love you without any judgment".

Another way of doing this exercise is by sitting at a quiet place and taking a big bowl filled with water in front of you. Now talk to the water, as you would talk to your best friend. Express all your emotions and feelings. Just let it out, whatever you are feeling at the moment. Once you feel that you are done with speaking, and nothing more is left to say. Carefully flush that water down the drain, without spilling it.

C) Forgiveness, let go, gratitude: इदं न मम   "Idam Na Mama" is a Sanskrit mantra. Translation: "This is not mine"- to let go which does not serve you anymore.

Forgiveness is a powerful step in clearing away emotional baggage from the past. When you forgive, you choose to let go of anger, hurt, and resentment that weigh you down. This doesn't mean you forget what happened or it was okay, but you free yourself from being tied to those negative emotions. Letting go helps you move forward with a lighter heart. It opens up space for more positive experiences and emotions. Forgiving isn't always easy, but it is a gift you give to yourself. By releasing past grievances, you pave the way for healing and peace within yourself, enhancing your overall well-being. It helps you to remain happy and content. If you clench yourself to the past, you will never be able to proceed towards the future. Letting go becomes easy when you clearly have the answer to this question:

Question: Do you want to let it go now or let it hurt me more?

*Answer:*____

____

____

____

Always remember healing, joy and peace always wait at the other side of letting go. Your choices define the direction of your life. You have to decide what you want to choose: "Letting go" or "holding on to your pain."

4

Roadmap from Victim to Victor

"Victory comes from never giving up. An indomitable fighting spirit, a flame that burns ever brighter in the face of obstacles, is what enables us to win."

- Daisaku Ikeda

Never give up on dreams of becoming who you want to be!! If you don't know what you are looking for, you are going to feel lost, not once, not twice but many times. so it is very important to ask yourself what am I looking for: is it social security, is it validation, is it name & fame, is it financial security, is it connection to my higher self/ my spiritual being, is it good mental and physical health, is it a harmonious family, is it my confidence in my ability to achieve my goals? It is important to bring CLARITY into your life and define your own definition of Success and Achievement based on your vision/role model/benchmark. Think about your passion, the actions that can drive you even at midnight. Now set your goals based on that and define the actions required to take you from your current moment to the moment of your vision. Live an inspired life.

It is a journey of going inward and taking all actions for self-growth. Your outer world is just a reflection of your inner world. So the moment you polish your inner self, the environment around you will start reflecting your inner beauty and will become a beautiful place to live in.

If you are following this book then by now, you would have got some clarity about your goals and the quality of life you want to create for yourself.

Forward pace in the future and see yourself, ask yourself the right questions-

- ❖ Why do I want whatever I want??
- ❖ What is aligned with my thought process, purpose and joy?
- ❖ Are you on autopilot?
- ❖ Whatever you chose to do because it was what you were "supposed" to do?
- ❖ What do you really want to do that you didn't allow yourself to do?
- ❖ What do you choose to do by default (like watching TV or being on social media)?
- ❖ What else could you be choosing to do instead?
- ❖ What do you actually WANT to do with your life?

Check if you are a person who speaks in your head:

I will do this when.....

I will travel the world when......

What if "When" never comes?? Think about it....

You have to make a conscious DECISION to stop welcoming all these 'whens'. Now is the time to make that choice.

When you are drowning in pain and suffering and holding yourself back, then you are the one who is suffering the most. So, it is better to bring yourself back from the suffering mode and begin the journey of self transformation.

<u>Table-8:</u>

GOAL/ Action			
	Levels		
What if I fail: If my business doesn't do well?	**Bad**	Loss	
		Gain	
	Worse	Loss	
		Gain	
	Worst	Loss	
		Gain	
What if I Succeed: If my business does well.	**Good**	Loss	
		Gain	
	Better	Loss	
		Gain	
	Best	Loss	
		Gain	.

Check for all the "What Ifs" holding you back from making inspired choices in life.

Write down the actions that you want to take but are not taking due to fear of failure. Please fill in the below table to get some facts out of your mind on a sheet of paper in black & white.

A sample is done for you:

GOAL/ Action			I want to start a business.
	Levels		
	Bad	Loss	I may not earn the expected profit.
		Gain	I will gain experience/ network/ satisfaction
What if I fail: If my business doesn't do well?	**Worse**	Loss	I may lose some money invested in business.
		Gain	I will gain experience of running a business.
	Worst	Loss	Loss of invested resources
		Gain	I will gain experience/ network/ satisfaction
	Good	Loss	Nothing
		Gain	My business will earn profit to recover my investments
What if I Succeed: If my business does well.	**Better**	Loss	Nothing
		Gain	My business will earn enough profit to continue my business.
	Best	Loss	Nothing
		Gain	My business will earn enough profit to expand my business.

Now the issue is - How can you make the process of change gradual and more sustaining? Rather than like many other projects in your life which you started but could never finish through discipline, adding step-by-step processes and getting adjusted to the changes.

Sometimes you don't take inspired actions unless you hit rock bottom. Let's understand the critical internal reasons holding you back.

Your scarcity mindset and limiting beliefs that support it:

A scarcity mindset is when you constantly feel like there isn't enough of something, whether it is money, time, or other resources. This way of thinking can make you feel anxious, limited, and overly competitive. While operating from a scarcity mindset, you may often worry about the limited number of opportunities and tend to lose what you already have. This might result in blocking your vision to appreciate what you currently have, further narrowing down your vision to focus on lack. This could further lead to a loss of hope for a better future. Scarcity perspective causes you to focus too much on what others have and what you lack, hence it is also known as a lacking mindset. It can keep you away from appreciating what you currently have and from sharing with others. A scarcity mindset hinders you from taking chances that would lead to exponential growth in life. Whereas, an abundance mindset is the attitude of believing that there's plenty for everyone, which leads to more happiness, generosity, and a sense of fulfillment. The scarcity mindset is developed when you operate from your limiting beliefs. You can shift from a scarcity mindset to an abundance mindset if you can break through your limiting beliefs.

A) Limiting beliefs- how to identify it:

Identifying your limiting beliefs starts with listening closely to your thoughts and noticing patterns. These are often the thoughts that pop up when you're about to try something new or challenging. In the beginning, you might feel, "I can't do this," "I'm not good enough," or "I don't deserve this." These feelings around your goal can help you identify limiting beliefs. To catch these beliefs, pay attention to moments when you feel stuck or when you're holding yourself back from doing something you want to do.

The below table is another tool to help you identify your limiting beliefs in a simplified manner, just remember to answer all the questions with utmost honesty.

Table-9:

Write your goal	How do you feel about it?	Is it achievable? (Yes/No)	If yes, then what actions need to be taken	Why do you feel that you cannot take this action?	Your limiting belief around your goal

A sample is done for your understanding:

Write your goal	How do you feel about it?	Is it achievable ? (Yes/No)	If yes, then what actions need to be taken	Why do you feel that you cannot take this action ?	Your limitin g belief around your goal
I want to run a successfu l business.	scare d	Yes	Arrange funds, gain skills to run a busines s	People will make fun of me if I fail.	I am not good enough .

B) Impact/influence of external factors in creating my limiting beliefs:

External factors play a big role in shaping your limiting beliefs. From a young age, messages from family, friends, teachers, and media can impact how you see yourself and your potential. For example, if you had often heard that making mistakes is bad, you might grow up fearing failure. Social media, too, can make you feel inadequate by constantly showing you images of 'perfect' lives. These outside influences can plant seeds of doubt, fear, and insecurity that limit your actions and goals. Recognizing that these beliefs might come from external sources rather than your eternal true nature can help you challenge and change them, freeing you to achieve more.

C) How can I transform limiting/ disempowering beliefs into empowering beliefs:

Transforming limiting beliefs into empowering ones begins with recognizing and challenging them and then replacing them with nurturing beliefs. First, identify the beliefs that hold you back, like "I can't succeed in this," and question their truth. Ask yourself, "Is this really true?" Look for evidence that contradicts these beliefs. For instance, recall past successes or strengths that demonstrate your capability. Next, replace negative beliefs with positive affirmations that reflect your abilities and worth, such as "I am capable of achieving great things." Repeat these affirmations regularly to reinforce them in your mind. Positive affirmations give you a sense of hope and faith that there is nothing that you cannot achieve. It is all about embracing your inner talent. Lastly, take small steps that align with your new beliefs, building confidence and proving your old beliefs wrong with each success.

Understanding and recognizing the limiting beliefs behind them is the first step towards transforming your reality. Once you see the connection between your feelings and what you believe about yourself, you can start to challenge those old limiting beliefs. For every such belief, ask yourself the following questions:

Question: Is it really true? Is it really valid now?

*Answer:*____

____

____

____

Question: What evidence do I have for this to be true now?

*Answer:*____

____

____

____

Question: If it is disempowering, then do I want to change it now?

*Answer:*____

____

____

____

Question: With which empowering belief/s do I want to replace it?

*Answer:*____

____

____

____

Question: *How do I want to see myself?*

Answer: ____

____

____

____

By questioning and eventually changing these beliefs, you can start to feel differently. This helps to break the emotional pattern and opens up a new way of seeing yourself and your situations.

Use the tools given in later chapters.

Your New Identity:

Your new identity is different from the earlier one as now you are someone who feels confident and content in your own skin. For example, my new identity is like this: "I strive to be kind, understanding, and supportive of others, treating everyone with respect and compassion. It is important to me to stay curious and eager to learn, always expanding my knowledge and skills. My aim is to be reliable and trustworthy, someone friends and family can count on. Ultimately, I want to lead a life where I can look back and feel proud of the positive impact I've had on those around me, contributing to my community and making a difference wherever I can." Similarly, you can define your new identity based on these clues.

Exercise: *Ask yourself this question: what do I want? If you really know what you want, that's really great. Start making a list of all your goals. But in case you don't get any answer, take a piece of paper and draw a vertical line in the center.*

On the left side of the paper write down what you don't want, then on the right side of the paper, write a counter statement. Ta-da, right side of the paper is your list of Goals that you want to achieve.

Keep that handy and prioritize it. Now choose the top 3 goals to work on with focus, refer to the last chapter to further work towards achieving your goals.

A) Who is your role model?:

Identifying a role model starts with figuring out who inspires you and why. Think about the people you admire, whether they're family members, teachers, celebrities, or historical figures. Consider what specific qualities or achievements draw you to them. Is it their kindness, bravery, intelligence, resilience or something else? Look for someone whose traits align with your values and goals. Once you've identified your role model, learn more about how they have achieved their success, faced challenges, and maintained their values. Understanding their journey can provide a blueprint for your own path, giving you motivation and guidance as you work towards your own aspirations. You can take inspiration from the actions they have taken to overcome challenges in their life. Their life model can help you in creating a framework for starting your journey.

B) Learn-Unlearn-Relearn:

Leave behind your old patterns of knowledge that are stopping you fulfilling your dreams. The concept of "learn, unlearn, relearn" is about staying flexible and adaptable in how you gather and update your knowledge. First, you learn new information or skills, absorbing what is taught or experienced. Then comes unlearning, which means letting go of outdated or incorrect information that you previously believed was true. This step is crucial because it clears the way for more accurate or efficient ways of thinking and doing things. Finally, relearning involves enhancing your knowledge by incorporating new, precise, and more pertinent information. This ongoing cycle is essential for staying up-to-date and effective in a rapidly changing world. This ongoing cycle is vital for being contemporary and effective in a rapidly changing world.

Powers that I already possess to achieve an abundance mindset:

An abundance mindset is the belief that there is plenty of everything in the world for everyone. It focuses on the possibilities and opportunities that exist, rather than limitations. People with an abundance mindset see life as full of potential for growth, success, and happiness. They are generous with others because they believe that sharing won't deplete their own resources. This mindset also helps individuals remain optimistic, even in tough times, because they trust that more good things can be created or achieved. Cultivating an abundance mindset involves shifting focus from what you lack to appreciating what you have and envisioning endless possibilities for the future.

A) Power of Choice:

Your greatest strength lies in your ability to choose. No matter the circumstances, you always have at least two options: to take action with determination or to yield to the situation. When life gets challenging, it may feel like there are no viable paths forward. Options may seem unattainable, or you might envision a route no one has taken before. Yet, this is precisely the moment to reclaim you power and explore all possible choices available to you. To fully utilize any power, it must be practiced. For example, to build muscle power, you need consistent exercise. Similarly, developing the mindset to fully embrace the power of choice requires actively seeking options at all times. This mindset fosters a proactive approach to life— one that focuses on success rather than being paralyzed by the fear of failure. Trusting in positive outcomes can profoundly influence your decisions and their outcomes.

This practice cultivates resilience and a "never give up" attitude, as you continually seek opportunities for growth instead of surrendering to life's challenges. According to the universal law of manifestation, the more opportunities will be created for you when you constantly look for it. As the poet and philosopher Rumi beautifully said, *"Whatever you seek is seeking you."* If you chose love, peace, joy, hope and success, life would present more opportunities filled with these positive experiences. On the other hand, choosing hopelessness, despair, hatred, or pessimism will draw more negativity into your life. So, what will you choose today to harness the power of choice wisely?

B) Power of support:

Leverage the power of support, means recognizing and utilizing the help and resources available from others around you. No one achieves success alone. When you tap into the support of friends, family, mentors, or colleagues, you amplify your ability to overcome challenges and reach your goals faster. This support can come in many forms: advice, encouragement, sharing of resources, or simply a listening ear. Actively seeking and accepting support not only eases your journey but also strengthens relationships and builds a network of reciprocal aid. Remember, asking for help is a sign of strength and a strategic move towards achieving your aspirations.

C) Power of subconscious mind:

People often fail to recognize the remarkable potential of the subconscious mind. It influences much of your daily lives, and your behaviors, from the habits you form to the emotions you feel. Your subconscious stores all your previous experiences and beliefs, guiding your actions and reactions without you even realizing it. You have the power to influence your subconscious in a positive way through techniques like visualization, affirmations, and mindful meditation. Nurturing a positive, solution-driven mindset conditions your subconscious to attract more positive outcomes in your life.

Tools and techniques to reveal

infinite potential

"Learn the techniques to open the Power of Your Heart, giving access to the infinite potential possibilities that truly exist for you."

— **Steven Redhead**

Unleash the Power of Your Heart and Mind

Now that you are in the last chapter of this book, congratulations to you for your determination to transform your life by leaps and bounds in the most positive manner. Before starting your journey of self-growth, you need to understand your starting point, i.e. your current reality. Below is the wheel of life, rate (on a scale of 1-10) your current life in all the areas given in this wheel of life.

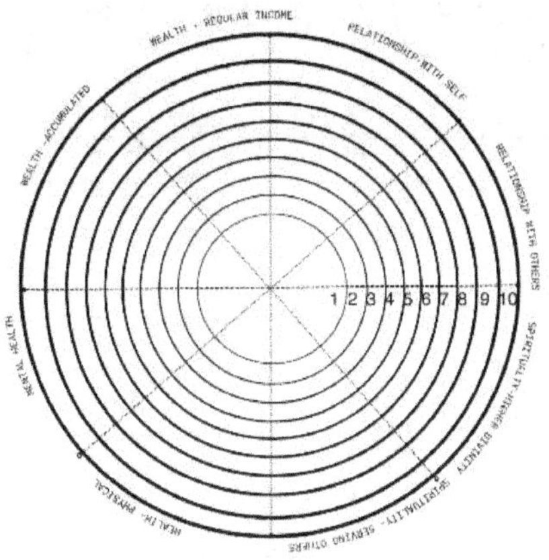

Now pick 3 areas having a rating of less than 5. These are the areas in your life which need your immediate attention. These three areas will define the direction in which you need to set your goals for achieving greater success in life. Put these three areas of life in the table given in this section.

In order to keep growing in life on the path that is aligned with your needs, you need to focus on the following three points:

A)   Dreams: Who Do You Really Want to Be?

Only "you" own your dreams. You only know what you want to achieve in life. The ultimate right way to live life lies in striving towards fulfilling your dreams joyfully. Your purpose as a human being is to bring joy in your life & in others' lives through your passion & dreams.

Sit quietly, ask yourself this question, and write down your answer:

Question: If nothing in this world could stop me, then what do I want to be?

Answer:_______________________________________

____

____

B)   Values: What Do You Value?

Your passions are the activities that fill your heart with joy instantly. These are the things that you can do for hours without getting tired. Time stops and you feel deeply engrossed when you do such activities. Based on your values and ideals about life you end up wanting the world to be better, in your own specific ways. Tuning into these greater values of your heart can unleash your infinite potential through the path of passion.

Sit quietly, ask yourself this question and write down your answer:

Question: How can I use my passion and talent to bring joy to someone else's life?

Answer:_______________________________________

____

____

The answer to these questions will help you to look for the right goal in life.

C) Commitment: How do you stay committed to living life with Integrity?

It is a common notion that it is not easy to live life when you stay committed to your passions and values. There could be distractions in all forms: limiting belief systems, social pressures, your own insecurities and vulnerabilities etc. But as Tony Robbins says, "Energy flows where focus goes". You have to make the choice, what do you want? When you follow your passions & values, your life condition elevates. You receive absolute joy by following your heart. Newer opportunities knock at your door if you stay committed to taking the right actions in the direction of your dreams and goals. When opportunity knocks, you just need to do one thing, grab them and utilize your full potential to achieve your desired goals.

Whenever you feel that you are digressing from your path, ask yourself these questions:

Question: Which aspects of my life I am committed to with my heart?

*Answer:*____

____

____

Question: What would it take for me to be living joyfully in sync with my talents, passion & values?

*Answer:*____

____

____

Answers to these questions and some of the other questions in the previous parts of this book will give you clarity of your vision and goals.

<u>Table-10:</u>

Areas of life	My dream	My Values	My commitment

Based on these exercises, pick your three major goals. Write your goals based on the actions that you are going to take and not just the "task" you want to accomplish. Do you need to adjust the way you've worded your goals?

Now, rewrite your goal(s) (1-3) based on outcomes:

*1.*____

*2.*____

*3.*____

We're all born with infinite potential and creativity. We all have it in us. Each and every one of us. That's the only truth

.- Deepak Chopra

After getting the clarity of your goals you can step by step follow the tools & techniques given in this chapter to consistently work towards achieving your goals.

Technique-1: 4D Method

This is a very simple method devised by me to achieve your desired goals, if you follow it step-by-step with honesty, you are bound to achieve your goals:

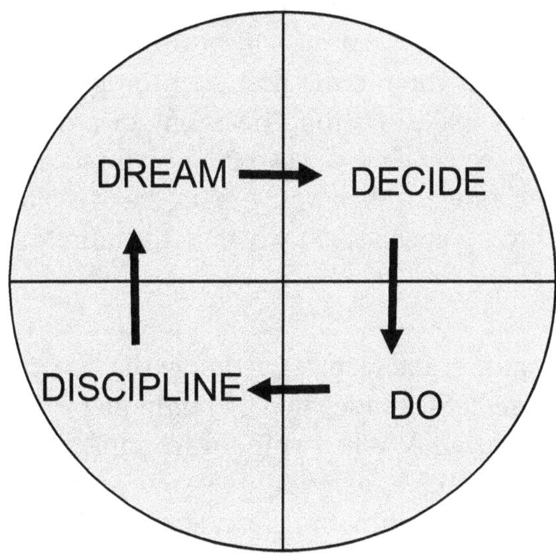

Dream:

From childhood to the last breath, you see a lot of dreams with your open eyes. You aspire to achieve different goals in different areas of life such as health, wealth, relationships and spirituality at different stages of life. Based on the circumstances, some areas take priority over others. All through life you have worked hard towards fulfilling your or your loved one's dreams. Your dreams have been the guiding light in living life. People who don't have any dreams or desires in life are the ones who live a life without purpose. That's like driving a car without knowing the destination. The journey to success starts with a dream, which is your desire to achieve something more in your life. Always dream bigger than what you can achieve. Have faith in the infinite potential that your life possesses.

Decide:

 Make a bold decision to pursue your dreams. Having dreams is good but working towards achieving them is much better. Strong determination is the first step towards victory. The moment you make a strong decision towards fulfilling a dream, every cell and nerve of your body will start filling with hope and courage. When you dream and visualize it as a reality, it gives you wings to fly high in the infinite sky.

Do:

Take appropriate and inspired action in the direction of your goal fulfillment. Stay motivated by reminding yourself of the "Why" of your goal. When you always remember that you want to achieve this goal to improve your condition of life in the desired area, then nothing can stop you from achieving that goal. No action is small if it is taking you closer to your goal. Some days would be there when you will not be able to take some considerable action towards achieving your goal. On those days ask yourself this question: what is the one small action that I can take towards my goal? Now you will not feel overwhelmed and now you will take that tiny action. Always remember that moving forward is necessary, even if by an inch.

Discipline:

Develop a discipline to make consistent efforts. The gap of a gifted talent can be filled through consistent efforts. It means, that even if you are not talented in any area, you are strongly determined to develop your skills, then you can do so by making diligent efforts consistently. Perfecting any skill requires daily practice and discipline of doing that task regularly. For example, all performing artists practice their art regularly, all sports persons practice in a disciplined way. Mastery comes through disciplined actions.

Table-11:

Dream	Decide	Do	Discipline
Sample: My dream is to become an author	I have decided to write a book.	I have prepared a detailed plan to write a book with detailed actionable points and I have started taking action on it with a deadline.	I have to make sure that I am consistent in making efforts towards achieving my dreams. I monitor my progress regularly and take corrective actions to persevere.

Technique-2 Increase vibration through Visualization

Harnessing the power of the subconscious mind and the law of attraction involves raising your vibration to attract desired outcomes. The idea is to insert the idea of your goal in your subconscious as if you have already received it. As soon as this is deep rooted in your subconscious mind, it will start manifesting in physical reality. By consistently aligning your vibration with positivity, you'll effortlessly attract opportunities and experiences aligned with your desires.

There are several ways to practice this and visualization is one of the methods to achieve your goals. Increasing vibration through visualization relates to quantum physics by tapping into the concept that everything in the universe is energy vibrating at different frequencies. To resonate with the higher frequencies of your desired physical reality, you must vibrate at those frequencies. When your life energy is depleted, you vibrate at a very low frequency. When you visualize positive outcomes or feelings, you emit coherent energy waves that resonate with similar frequencies in the quantum field. Focusing on what you desire or how you want to feel, causes your thoughts and emotions to resonate at higher frequencies. You align your thoughts and emotions with higher frequencies.

By aligning your thoughts and emotions with higher vibrations through visualization, you influence the quantum field, potentially attracting experiences and opportunities that match your focused intentions, thus shaping your reality. Increasing vibration through visualization involves picturing positive outcomes or feelings in your mind's eye. This practice can elevate your mood, attract similar energies, and manifest your goals more effectively. Visualizing success, love, or happiness creates a powerful mental state that resonates with the universe, enhancing your overall positivity and attracting opportunities that match your aspirations. It is a simple yet potent way to harness the law of attraction and boost your spiritual and emotional well-being.

Technique-3: "Ta-Da" List:

This is your "To-do" list of all action items. Why do we call it a "ta-da" list? "To-do" sounds like an unpleasant list of tasks that you have to do, while "ta-da" is more inspirational. Every time we finish a task, we cross it off and say "ta-da!" Celebrating even the little victories gives us a sense of accomplishment and builds momentum. We enjoy it so much, in fact, that if we find that we've completed a task that we didn't already have on our list, we ADD IT to the list just so we can cross it off! Accomplishing targets gives us a sense of achievement and motivates us to do more.

Take the Priority 1 items from your Monthly Plan and write them down as Actionable Tasks. If needed, break tasks even further into action steps.

IDENTIFY TASKS: Take the #1 priorities you identified for your monthly plan. Break down these tasks further into action points for everyday.

PRIORITIZE: Identify which tasks are a priority (mark 1 through 3) and plan to do level-1 FIRST.

PLAN: If necessary, assign time-framed tasks to the schedule and allocate other tasks to specific days of the week. Make sure to keep your weekly list in a convenient location for easy reference when setting daily goals.

- If items need to be completed on a specific day, mark it on your planner.

- If items are priorities that absolutely must be completed this week, star or highlight them

- and focus on these FIRST.

- As you accomplish things, cross them off. Keep them there to show you what you've

- Done! Ta-da!

- Remember that sometimes life happens and not everything on your list for the week will happen. That's okay, simply move it forward to next week!

Create Your Daily Plan:

Every day, look at what you have on your Schedule as well as your weekly Ta-Da list. Write in your sub-goals/tasks for the day and then IGNORE EVERYTHING ELSE.

So what are your today's Tasks (in order of priority)

1.____

2.____

3.____

Technique-4: Time management (matrix of important/urgent task list):

Time management helps you achieve your goals by allowing you to focus on what's important. By prioritizing tasks, you can ensure that essential activities get done first. This reduces procrastination, increases productivity and provides a better work-life balance. Setting clear goals and deadlines keeps you motivated and on track. Effective time management also helps you avoid last-minute rushes and stress, leading to better quality work. Overall, it ensures that you make steady progress towards your goals, making them more attainable and less overwhelming. Below is a tool- Eisenhower Matrix (credited to the task management system of US President Dwight Eisenhower)

Benefits –

1. Prioritizing complex or unclear issues becomes easier.

2. It offers a fast and simple, yet reliable way to assess choices.

3. It can be customized for different priority setting requirements, including projects, services, personal tasks, and more.

How to use it:

After setting your goal you need to identify Urgent and Important tasks:

- Urgent tasks require your immediate attention. These tasks put you in a hurried mindset & generate stress.

- Important tasks help you achieve long-term goals. To know what things are actually important, you first have to figure out your own goals.

Quadrants of the Eisenhower Matrix:

Quadrant I (Important and Urgent)-

These are the activities that you have to do right away: crises, problems, or deadlines. There could be two types of Important & urgent tasks-

1. Type-1: Tasks arised due to some unexpected/ unplanned/ unforeseen/ sudden situations/ accidents/ emergencies. ex. Accidents, pandemics, sudden changes in plans etc.

2. Type-2: Tasks, which were earlier in Q-II and got delayed until they become urgent. ex. waiting for the last minute to submit a report, delayed bill payment etc.

The best way to handle Type-1 tasks is to do the action required at that time with calmness and patience by utilizing all the existing resources. You can reduce the Type-2 tasks, by completing them well within the deadline through proper planning.

Quadrant II (Important and Not Urgent)-

These are tasks that help you stay focused to achieve long-term goals but do not have a pressing deadline (ex. studying for an exam in two weeks). These tasks can move to Quadrant I if not completed in a timely manner. It is important to first take care of Quadrant I and then Quadrant II. Quadrant II tasks can be planned over a while. Avoid stress & poor work quality by completing these tasks before they move to Quadrant I.

Quadrant III (Not Important and Urgent)-

These tasks require your attention right now but do not help you achieve your goals on an immediate basis. These tasks look like interruptions from other people or favors; they're often time-consuming. They are not necessarily bad, but they need to be balanced with activities from Quadrants I and II. The solution is to become more assertive and see how these tasks can be delegated.

Quadrant IV (Not Important and Not Urgent) –

These tasks are mostly distractions and could take up most of the day if not moderated. These activities do not have to be eliminated but should be pushed until other important tasks are completed. After a busy day, watching TV or going on social media can help you relax. Just make sure that they are done in a controlled manner so that they do not consume the time and energy required to complete tasks of Q-I & Q-II.

Bonus (for tech savvy readers)- suggested list of apps for Time Management/time tracking (Please use your discretion before using it): Todoist, Workflow, Toggl Track, HourStack, Timely, Memtime, TrackingTime, RescueTime etc.

Technique-5: Daily rituals:

Daily rituals are the framework of your life, shaping routines that anchor you amidst chaos. They may vary from person to person depending upon individual preferences and ease. All successful people have a strong and disciplined daily routine. Some find solace in meditation, others in a brisk morning jog or exercising. These daily rituals give you a fresh start every day to live each day in the most meaningful ways. It sets the tone to stitch together the fabric of your existence, providing comfort, structure, and meaning in the rhythm of everyday life. It helps you to remain disciplined by letting good habits enter into your lives and begin your day with vibrance and zeal.

A) Gratitude/journaling:

Utilize the power of gratitude and journaling to elevate your vibration and attract positivity. Start each day by writing down three things you're grateful for, fostering an appreciation and abundance mindset. Reflect on experiences that bring joy, love, and growth, reinforcing positive emotions. Incorporate affirmations of gratitude into your daily routine, affirming blessings and abundance. Journal about moments of gratitude throughout the day, amplifying their impact. As you cultivate gratitude, you'll notice an energy shift, attracting more blessings and opportunities into your life. Consistent practice of gratitude journaling magnifies positivity, raising your vibration to align with abundance and fulfillment.

Gratitude goes beyond mere emotion; it embodies an energy, a vibration that harmonizes with the universe's inherent abundance. Try to use "Thank you" as a mantra and repeat it as many times as you can. The more you repeat the phrase, "Thank you", the more opportunities you will receive to be grateful for.

When you authentically practice gratitude, you resonate at a frequency that draws in more blessings, opportunities, and positivity. It is akin to tuning into your preferred radio station: the clearer the signal, the stronger the reception. By cultivating a gratitude mindset, you're not merely saying 'thank you'; it is about syncing with a universal wavelength, thereby enhancing the ease and joy in transforming your dreams into reality.

Exercises:

1.   Every morning as soon as you wake up, please say "Thank you" to the universe/ creator/God (whatever resonates with your way of life philosophy) for a minimum of 5 things. For example: every morning, you can thank the Universe for having wonderful experiences as a human in this lifetime. You can be grateful for your life, family, peace, good health, food, nature's love etc. This looks like a very simple technique, but if you do it with full faith, it has the power to increase your vibrations quickly. It helps to give you an instant energy boost to start your day at a high energy level.

2.   Gratitude Journaling: Everyday before going to bed, write down three things you're grateful for that have happened during the day. Feel the warmth of gratitude envelop you, and observe how this simple practice transforms your life. When you bestow gratitude towards others, happiness comes to you manifold.

Example:

Date:

Today I am happy and grateful for:

1.____

____

2.____

____

3.____

____

#Bonus (for tech savvy readers)- suggested list of apps for Gratitude (Please use your discretion before using it): Gratitude Garden, Gratitude Journal – Private Diary & Daily Quotes, 365 Gratitude — Daily Reading, Delightful, Three Good Things, Spark, Presently, 5 Minute Journal etc.

B) Affirmations:

In simpler words, affirmation means to accept as true/ to agree/ to give consent to. As per my book: "Everything about affirmations"- affirmations are the way to give your consent to the idea that you want to manifest or create in your life. The power of affirmation is essentially the infinite potential that lies within your own lives. Whatever statement you think, hear, speak, read, or write about life is an affirmation. Whatever you experience with your five senses—taste, smell, hearing, touch, and vision—becomes an affirmation when you experience the emotions associated with it. You can use the power of positive affirmations to transform your "current reality" into "desired reality". While using the power of affirmations, you constantly feed your subconscious mind with positive and empowering thoughts related to your goals/ desired reality. This in turn helps in creating reality through the energy and vibrations of your thoughts and emotions that flow across the entire universe through your physical body.

Affirmations can be used in all areas of life that affect your mental and physical well-being. You can manifest an abundance of Health, Wealth, Relationships, Love, Success, Peace, Hope, Courage, and Career in your life by using the immense power of affirmations. This also helps in improving self-esteem, overcoming fears and anxieties, achieving goals, and fostering inner peace and happiness.

Affirmations are powerful tools for controlling the subconscious mind and the law of attraction. Choose affirmations that are consistent with your goals and desires, and write them in the present tense with positivity and conviction. Repeat your affirmations every day, preferably in the morning or before bed, to profoundly imprint them on your subconscious. Visualize yourself already experiencing the reality depicted in your affirmations, infusing them with emotion and belief.

Consistency and faith are the keys to manifest through affirmations; reinforce your affirmations regularly to overwrite any negative beliefs or doubts. Trust in the process, knowing that affirmations program your subconscious to attract opportunities and experiences aligned with your desires. Further, you can read my book "Everything About Affirmations" to get in depth knowledge about how to take advantage of the power of affirmations in your life.

Exercise: Please choose the right affirmations from the area of your life that you want to transform, and then write affirmations 11 times every day. Suppose you want to manifest business success with an income of $10,000, then your affirmations would be: "I am happy and grateful for *my successful business earning $10,000 per month, thank you, thank you, thank you."*

C) Vision board:

Utilize a vision board to leverage the power of the subconscious mind and the law of attraction effectively. Begin by gathering images, words, and symbols representing your desired goals and aspirations. Arrange them on a board in a visually appealing way. Place your vision board where you can see it daily, allowing your subconscious to absorb the images and align with your intentions. Visualize yourself achieving each goal with clarity and emotion while focusing on gratitude. Regularly review and update your vision board to keep it relevant and inspiring. By consistently engaging with your vision board, you'll manifest your dreams with the power of attraction. There are many simple ways to create your vision board:

1. You can create it on a computer using simple software like documents or spreadsheets, by searching & putting all the relevant pics from the internet/ personal photo archive, in one document. Then use it as a desktop wallpaper, so that you can see it most of the time. You can also take a coloured printout of this and paste it near a place which you visit most of the time of the day, like your bed, workplace, desk, refrigerator etc.

2. Or you can cut relevant pics from magazines and paste it on a big sheet to make your vision board.

3. You can also use a digital copy of your vision board to make wallpaper of your mobile so that you can see it all the time.

4. There are many apps available now to create a vision board on mobile.

Bonus (for tech-savvy readers)- suggested list of apps for Vision board (Please use your discretion before using it): Visionboard2024, VISUAPP, Vision Board - Perfectly Happy, Corkulous - Your Ideas, Subliminal Vision Boards, Sparkello - Vision Board, iwish etc.

D) Mirror Exercise: Mirror exercise is the simplest exercise to increase self-confidence and self-love. Let me ask a few simple questions:

Question: How do you feel when you look at yourself in the mirror?

Answer:____

____

Question: Do you admire yourself or do you focus on your flaws?

Answer:____

____

Sometimes when you lose self-respect & self-confidence then it takes a lot of courage to look deep into your own eyes with confidence and say to yourself these magical words: "I love you".

Have you ever wondered, If you do not accept yourself unconditionally as it is then who else will do it?

Self-love is something that needs to be practiced daily, to let it go into your subconscious level. This will help you to operate from a place of self-love. When you start embracing yourself, peacefully drop all judgements against yourself and others. So how can you start loving yourself? Try the daily self-love exercise called the "Mirror exercise" to help you focus on the positive. The mirror exercise, popularized by self-help author Louise Hay, is a powerful technique for building self-esteem and fostering a positive self-image. It involves standing in front of a mirror, looking directly into your own eyes, and affirming positive statements about yourself. Typically, you start by saying your name followed by affirmations like "I love you" or "I accept you exactly as you are." The practice encourages direct engagement with self-perception, confronting negative beliefs and replacing them with affirming, compassionate views towards oneself. This exercise can be deeply emotional and transformative, helping to reinforce self-love and acceptance over time, which are critical for personal growth and happiness.

The next time you are in front of a mirror, look yourself in the eye, smile, and say something positive like the examples below:
"I look good today!"
"I am enough."
"I am strong."

"I can handle this."
"I am amazing."
"I am thankful to be alive."

Practicing self-love means treating yourself with the same kindness and respect that you give to others or expect from others. It involves recognizing your own worth and taking care of your well-being. This can mean setting aside time for activities that you enjoy, saying no when you're overwhelmed, and forgiving yourself for your mistakes. It also includes speaking positively about yourself and replacing self-criticism with encouragement. Practicing self-love isn't selfish; it is essential for mental and emotional health. By valuing yourself, you set a healthy standard for how others should treat you and strengthen your relationships. There is a thin line of difference between self-love and selfishness. When you fill yourself with love, only then you will be able to pour out what you behold beneath. Start small, like taking a few moments each day to acknowledge something you appreciate about yourself. Choose yourself above all the miseries around you!

Dear Reader, now you are equipped with all the tools and techniques to begin your amazing journey of  knowing yourself a little better, loving yourself and transforming all your dreams into reality.

It is never too late, so don't hesitate any longer; start using techniques that are aligned with your distinctive individuality.

My prayers and best wishes are always with you.

Yes, You Can Do It!!

Sending you the light of love, joy and peace,

Mandvi

End

www.ingramcontent.com/pod-product-compliance
Lightning Source LLC
LaVergne TN
LVHW020924200726
843506LV00011B/1812